SING A SONG OF SEASONS

Illustrated by SALLY GREGORY

Compiled by Linda M. Jennings

HODDER AND STOUGHTON
LONDON SYDNEY AUCKLAND TORONTO

Thoughts for a Cold Day

A little bit of blowing,
A little bit of snow,
A little bit of growing,
And crocuses will show.
On every twig that's lonely
A new green leaf will spring,
On every patient tree-top
A thrush will stop and sing.

Anon.

A Change in the Year

It is the first mild day of March:
　　Each minute sweeter than before,
The redbreast sings from the tall larch
　　That stands beside our door.

There is a blessing in the air,
　　Which seems a sense of joy to yield
To the bare trees, and mountains bare,
　　And grass in the green field.

William Wordsworth

Spring

Sound the flute!
Now it's mute.
Birds delight
Day and Night;
Nightingale
In the dale,
Lark in Sky,
Merrily,
Merrily, merrily, to welcome in the Year.

Little Boy,
Full of joy;
Little Girl,
Sweet and small;
Cock does crow,

So do you;
Merry voice,
Infant noise,
Merrily, merrily, to welcome in the Year.

Little Lamb,
Here I am;
Come and lick
My white neck;
Let me pull
Your soft Wool;
Let me kiss
Your soft face;
Merrily, merrily, we welcome in the Year.

William Blake

Pippa's Song

The year's at the spring;
And day's at the morn;
Morning's at seven;
The hillside's dew-pearled;
The lark's on the wing;
The snail's on the thorn:
God's in his heaven —
All's right with the world!

Robert Browning

Bluebells

The breeze is on the bluebells,
The wind is on the lea;
Stay out! Stay out! my little lad,
And chase the wind with me.
If you will give yourself to me
Within the fairy ring,
At dead midnight,
When stars are bright,
You'll hear the bluebells sing.

Juliana Horatia Ewing

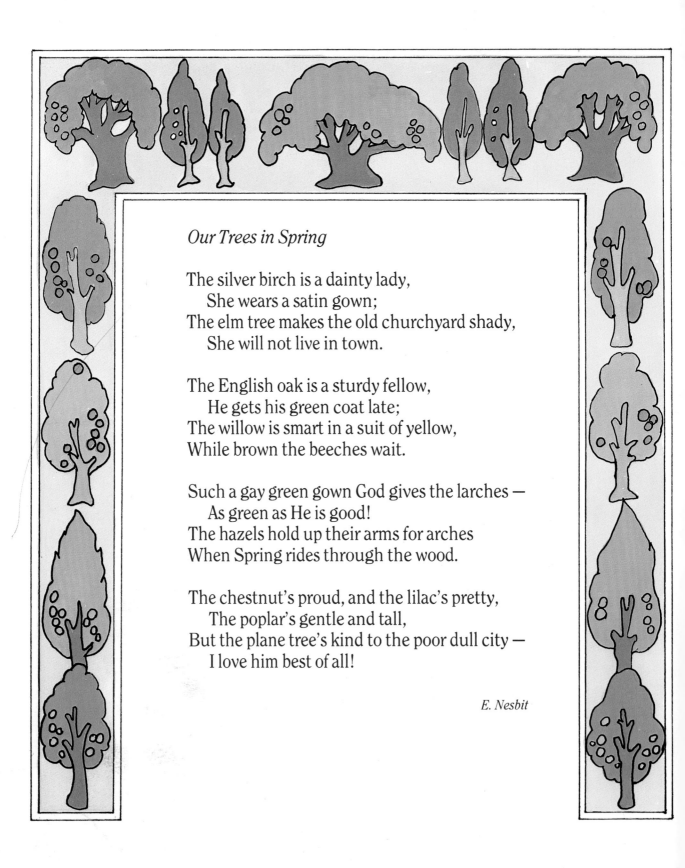

Our Trees in Spring

The silver birch is a dainty lady,
   She wears a satin gown;
The elm tree makes the old churchyard shady,
   She will not live in town.

The English oak is a sturdy fellow,
   He gets his green coat late;
The willow is smart in a suit of yellow,
While brown the beeches wait.

Such a gay green gown God gives the larches —
   As green as He is good!
The hazels hold up their arms for arches
When Spring rides through the wood.

The chestnut's proud, and the lilac's pretty,
   The poplar's gentle and tall,
But the plane tree's kind to the poor dull city —
   I love him best of all!

E. Nesbit

Here we come a-piping
In spring-time and in May;
Green fruit a-ripening,
And winter fled away.
The Queen she sits upon the strand,
Fair as a lily, white as wand;
Seven billows on the sea,
Horses riding fast and free,
And bells beyond the sand.

Anon.

Summer Evening

The sandy cat by the Farmer's chair
Mews at his knee for dainty fare;
Old Rover in his moss-greened house
Mumbles a bone, and barks at a mouse.
In the dewy fields the cattle lie
Chewing the cud 'neath a fading sky;
Dobbin at manger pulls his hay:
Gone is another summer's day.

Walter de la Mare

Full early in the morning
Awakes the summer sun.
The month of June arriving,
The cold and night are done.
The cuckoo is a fine bird,
She whistles as she flies,
And as she whistles "cuckoo",
The bluer grow the skies.

Anon.

In the Fair Forest

In Summer when the woods are green
    And leaves are large and long,
Full merry it is in the fair forest
    To hear the small birds' song.

To see the red deer seek the dale
    And leave the hills so high,
To shade themselves among the glades
    Under the greenwood tree.

Old ballad

Rain in Summer

How beautiful is the rain!
After the dust and heat,
In the broad and fiery street,
In the narrow lane,
How beautiful is the rain!

How it clatters along the roofs,
Like the tramp of hoofs.
How it gushes and struggles out
From the throat of the overflowing spout!

Across the window pane
It pours and pours;
And swift and wide,
With a muddy tide,
Like a river down the gutter roars
The rain, the welcome rain!

H. W. Longfellow

Bed in Summer

In winter I get up at night
And dress by yellow candle-light.
In summer, quite the other way,
I have to go to bed by day.

I have to go to bed and see
The birds still hopping on the tree,
Or hear the grown-up people's feet
Still going past me in the street.

And does it not seem hard to you,
When all the sky is clear and blue,
And I should like so much to play,
To have to go to bed by day?

R. L. Stevenson

August Afternoon

Where shall we go?
What shall we play?
What shall we do
On a hot summer day?

We'll sit on the swing.
Go low. Go high.
And drink lemonade
Till the glass is dry.

One straw for you,
One straw for me,
In the cool green shade
Of the walnut tree.

Marion Edey

Harvest Rhyme

Harvest home! Harvest home!
The boughs do shake and the bells do ring,
So merrily comes our harvest in,
Our harvest in, our harvest in,
So merrily comes our harvest in.

Well ploughed, well sown,
Well reaped, well mown,
Never a load over-thrown,
Why shouldn't we sing harvest home!

Anon.

J is for Jam

Blackberries on the brambles!
Winnie cries, "Here I am."
And through the thicket she scrambles,
To pick the berries for jam.

And soon she has torn her pinny,
And scratched her face, poor lamb.
But what does it matter to Winnie
When she's picking berries for jam?

And soon, oh soon (need you ask it?)
The berries her small mouth cram.
She brings home an empty basket,
But she's full of blackberry jam.

Eleanor Farjeon

Autumn Fires

In the other gardens
   And all up the vale,
From the autumn bonfires
   See the smoke trail!

Pleasant summer over,
   And all the summer flowers,
The red fire blazes,
   The grey smoke towers.

Sing a song of seasons!
   Something bright in all!
Flowers in the summer,
   Fires in the fall!

R. L. Stevenson

Autumn

I love the fitful gust that shakes
   The casement all the day,
And from the glossy elm tree takes
   The faded leaves away,
Twirling them by the window pane
With thousand others down the lane.

I love to see the shaking twig
   Dance till the shut of eve,
The sparrow on the cottage rig,
   Whose chirp would make believe
That Spring was just now flirting by
In Summer's lap with flowers to lie.

I love to see the cottage smoke
   Curl upwards through the trees;
The pigeons nestled round the cote
   On November days like these;
The cock upon the dunghill crowing,
The mill sails on the heath a-going.

The feather from the raven's breast
   Falls on the stubble lea;
The acorns near the old crow's nest
   Fall pattering down the tree;
The grunting pigs that wait for all,
Scramble and hurry where they fall.

John Clare

Weathers

This is the weather the cuckoo likes,
    And so do I;
When showers betumble the chestnut spikes,
    And nestlings fly:
And the little brown nightingale bills his best,
And they sit outside at "The Travellers' Rest",
And maids come forth sprig-muslin drest,
And citizens dream of the south and west,
    And so do I.

This is the weather the shepherd shuns,
    And so do I;
When beeches drip in browns and duns,
    And thresh and ply;
And hill-hid tides throb, throe on throe,
And meadow rivulets overflow,
And drops on gate-bars hang in a row,
And rooks in families homeward go,
And so do I.

Thomas Hardy

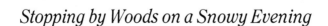

Stopping by Woods on a Snowy Evening

Whose woods these are I think I know.
His house is in the village, though;
He will not see me stopping here
To watch his woods fill up with snow.

My little horse must think it queer
To stop without a farmhouse near
Between the woods and frozen lake
The darkest evening of the year.

He gives his harness bells a shake
To ask if there is some mistake.
The only other sound's the sweep
Of easy wind and downy flake.

The woods are lovely, dark and deep,
But I have promises to keep,
And miles to go before I sleep,
And miles to go before I sleep.

Robert Frost

I will keep Christmas

I will keep Christmas in the cold hedgerow,
With red shining holly and winter snow.
I will keep Christmas far from any town
On the frosted side of the windswept down.

Stars will be candles of sweet silver fire,
Swinging at midnight over tree and spire,
Waves will be booming bells and break the air,
With glory and greeting and winged prayer.

I will keep Christmas alone and away,
Praising the Lord of all on Christmas Day.

P. A. Ropes

Acknowledgments

The Editor and Publishers are grateful to the following for the use of copyright material:

The Literary Trustees of Walter de la Mare and the Society of Authors as their representative for 'Summer Evening' by Walter de la Mare from *Peacock Pie* published by Faber & Faber Ltd: Charles Scribner's Sons for 'August Afternoon' by Marion Edey and Dorothy Grider from *Open the Door: Rhymes for Children:* David Higham Associates Limited for 'J is for Jam' by Eleanor Farjeon from *Invitation to a Mouse* published by Pelham Books: The Estate of Robert Frost and Jonathan Cape Ltd for 'Stopping by Woods on a Snowy Evening' from *The Poetry of Robert Frost* edited by Edward Connery Lathem: and Bell and Hyman Ltd for 'I will Keep Christmas' by P. A. Ropes from *The Book of 1000 Poems* published by Evans Brothers.